Griffin's Day in the Milky Way

...and more poetic tales

Suchitra Bapat

BookLeaf Publishing

India | USA | UK

Presentation by *BookLeaf Publishing*

Web: www.bookleafpub.com

E-mail: info@bookleafpub.com

ISBN: 9789360949716

First edition 2024

*Dedicated to my Mum with
everlasting love and gratitude*

ACKNOWLEDGEMENTS

A big thank you to the team at BookLeaf Publishing for providing this platform and all the help that this book needed to get to its feet. Shivani, Lavleen and Shikha, I couldn't have done it without you!

The illustrations in the book are by Esha Singh. Esha perfectly captured the essence of each poem and depicted it beautifully. The endearing ponytails, quizzical expressions, and little details in the illustrations stole my heart and completely changed the feel of the book. Thank you so much Esha!

I must express my heartfelt gratitude to my father Shrikrishna Bapat. He has consistently supported my every idea and undertaking and this project was no exception. From patiently listening to each poem, to debating about the cover design with me, he has been there from start to end. Thank you, Papa, for your belief and confidence in me always.

A huge thank you goes out to my husband and best friend, Samir. One glance at his face while reading a poem provided invaluable feedback! His loud guffaws when he found something funny, his candid criticism when something needed refining and his witty title suggestions played a crucial role in bringing the book to life!

Diya and Vivaan, my children, are the true inspiration behind these verses. Their unique perspectives, genuine smiles, at times puzzled expressions, and suggestions greatly influenced the narrative and wording of the poems! Of course, not to mention, that they felt targeted in most of them!

My dedicated writing time was 6:30 am, a peaceful hour when the household was still asleep. I want to say a big thank you to my mother-in-law Manisha Joshi, for it was then, that she would prepare a steaming cup of tea, ready to listen to my verses and offer unwavering encouragement to keep going.

I am eternally indebted to Mitali, my cousin, friend and confidante. A wonderful writer and poet, she spent so much time reviewing every poem and making immensely valuable suggestions to improve the metre, the rhyme and the feel.

It was so much fun to share this with my friends Aabha, Kalyani and Shweta. They were as excited as me when I started, read and commented on all the poems, rated them in order of liking, made title suggestions and made the whole experience even more enjoyable and fun!

Anuja, my cousin and colleague, thank you so much for listening to the poems and designing the first look of the book cover!

And a big thank you to all the folks that I randomly read poems out to, to get feedback and suggestions!

As I bring this to a close, I want to thank my mother, who is no longer with us, from the bottom of my heart. She was a lover of English puns and wordplay, an avid scrabble player, and she would have enjoyed this project immensely. Mamma, I missed you and thought of you every step of the way, imagining fun, yet insightful reviews with you. I hope you can see the words I've written, and I dedicate this book to you, with everlasting love and gratitude.

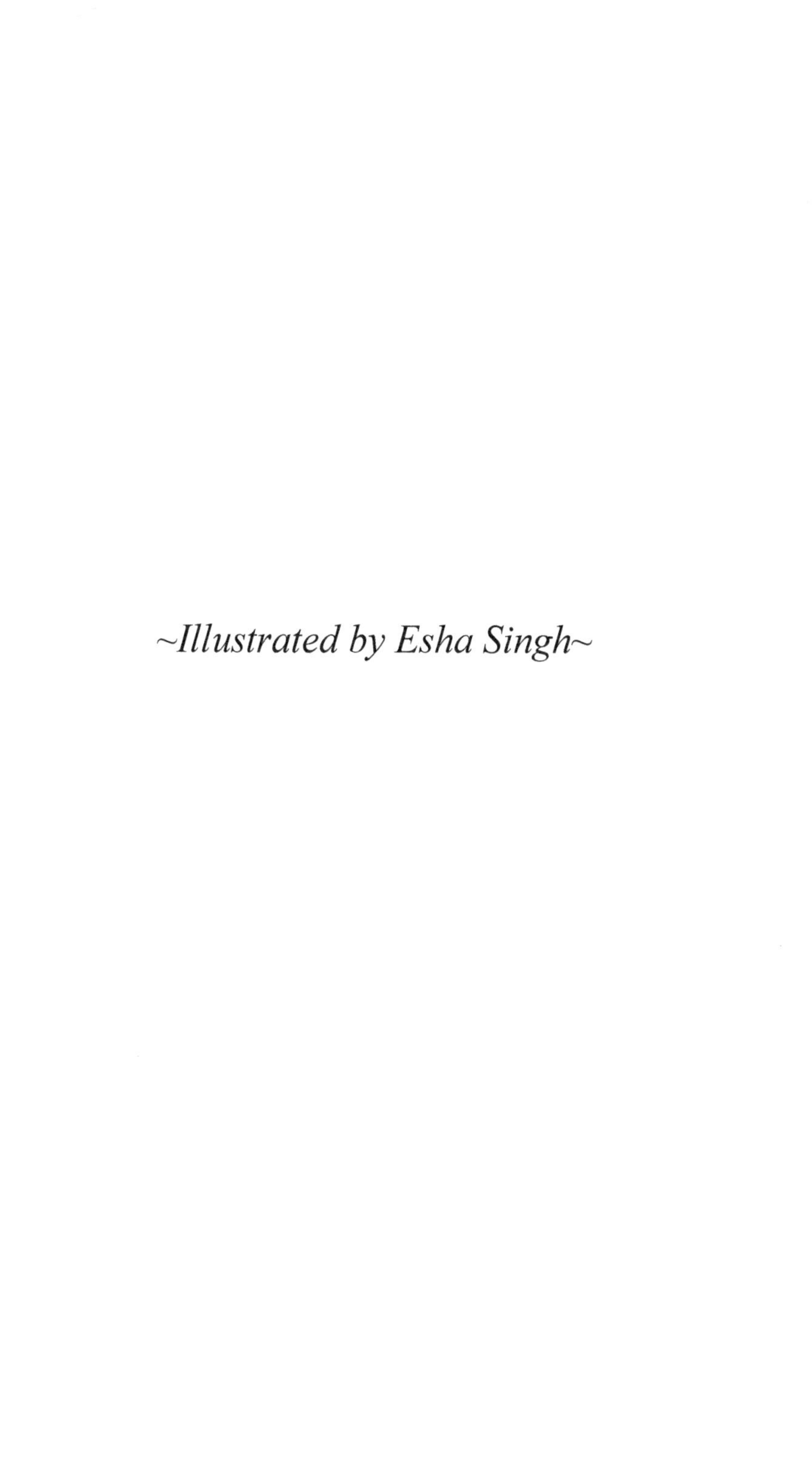

~Illustrated by Esha Singh~

PREFACE

Welcome to a world where laughter lingers in the little things, where humour finds a home in the humdrum of everyday family life. This collection of 21 light-hearted poems is an ode to the amusing moments that pepper our days but often go unnoticed.

From the quirky to the whimsical, these verses celebrate the delightful absurdities and events that make life unexpectedly entertaining. As you turn these pages, may you find yourself nodding in recognition, and rediscovering the simple pleasure of a well-timed joke or a clever rhyme.

Happy reading, and may these poems bring a smile to your face and a chuckle to your heart.

TABLE OF CONTENTS

Griffin's Day in the Milky Way

Have you heard of a grasshopper called Griffin?
He had a power that caused a sensation!
He could close his eyes and think of a place,
And then jump to that very destination!

He loved the hot, dry summer,
He could tolerate a smattering of cold.
But with all his heart he loathed the rain,
Thunder clouds, he could not behold.

And then one day it happened,
After days of the blazing sun,
The pouring rain pelted down.
Drenching everything and everyone.

Griffin crouched under a leaf.
He was miserable, cold and wet.
He cursed the weather and thought to himself,
"If only I could get off this planet!"

And then suddenly, realisation struck,
This planet, of course he could flee,
He closed his eyes, concentrated hard,
And then jumped straight to Mercury.

He landed on a surface, hard and rocky,
But the second it touched his feet,
He needed to jump, to be airborne again,
Because of the unforgiving, scorching heat!

The sun was too close, that was obvious,
So once more he took flight.
But just as he approached Venus,
He was blinded by a dazzling light.

Venus has a cover of clouds,
As thick as thick can be,
That reflects all the light away,
Making it the second brightest object you see!

Confused and flustered by this bright planet,
But still wanting to get away from ours,
Griffin the grasshopper stayed in flight,
And extended his jump to Mars.

Mars loomed large, looking red and rusty,
Winds were blowing hard, making the air very
dusty,
Griffin pondered for a moment, on why it looked
so red,
It is because of the rust present in its soil bed.

By now Griffin was starting to get, just a wee bit
thirsty.
He also felt the temperature, dropping to a lower
degree.
He wondered how it was possible, how could it
be?
That a planet so close to our warm Earth, could
get so very chilly!

He paused to think about Jupiter.
A quick spinning planet, made of gas, should he
even consider?
Would he get dizzy and what should he do,
If his feet found no ground, and he just fell
through?

Saturn seemed intriguing, the rings too, seemed
nice.
But to go through them, he would have to brave
rocks, dust and ice.
On Uranus and Neptune he would surely freeze,

The foul gas would make it very difficult to
breathe.

Now his options were limited; to this fact he did
surrender,
That back home, Earth, he would have to enter.
He would find water, warmth and something to
eat,
So he closed his eyes and made the leap.

The air was balmy and cool, after the recent rain.
It felt so good to be among familiar nature again.
And his tired feet rested, at long last,
Where he loved to hop the most—on the lush
green grass!

The Procrasti-nots

Nitya was a lovely girl, bright, sensitive and
kind,
The only thing she could not do was finish
things on time!
She was always excited about an idea; would
never whine or groan,
But when it came to taking action, she would
always postpone!

Now Nitya had a weakness, a weakness for
shoes.
She had recently seen a shop that was quite new!
So on one Saturday, when her dad was free,
She decided to take him on a shopping spree!

The shop was peculiar, different from where she had been,
Some of the shoes had names! She even thought that some could see!
A pair of boots was calling to her, itching to be bought,
The salesman told her that their name was The PROCRASTI-NOTS!

Her dad raised an eyebrow, but she thought that was cool,
She wanted to show them off to her friends from school!
She was so excited that she wore them then and there!
But she found it a little weird, when they almost wore themselves!

She walked into her house, flung her bags on the bed!
Her dad asked her to pick them up, "Later," she said.
Suddenly the boots tightened, around her feet in bands!
She simply couldn't help it, she just had to stand!

Her feet seemed to be moving entirely on their
own!
They took her to the bed, where the bags were
thrown!
And there she was rooted, her feet made her
stay!
Until she picked up the bags, to put them right
away!

She was unnerved, shaken and shocked!
She tried to take the boots off, but she just could
not!

Since it was Saturday, she had homework to do!
Solve some Maths questions, read a page or two.
She thought of the time she had, the whole day
lay ahead!
So she picked up a book and started reading it
instead!

Suddenly it started, that tight, tingling feeling!
Before it got worse, she threw down what she
was reading!
But the boots grew tighter and walked her to her
table!
Until, to do her homework, she was ready and
able!

She was infuriated, but not very shocked!
When she just could not take off, the
Procrasti-nots!

She had to write a note, to thank a good friend.
And without any delay, she picked up a pen.
As she wrote the note, and got done with it,
She felt the boots loosen; just a little bit!

Now, with Nitya, if you have some work to do,
I assure you, that wait, you will not have to!
As for those boots, they're up on a rack.
She doesn't look up, she's afraid they'll glare
back!

Don't Ask Me
What I Want To Be

When grown-ups come over for dinner or tea,
There is a question that they always ask me!
It comes without warning and quite suddenly.
When I grow up, what I want to be!

To think about this, I've had no time!
I've been playing, having fun, such a busy life!
To answer, "I don't know," would be rather
silly.
So my mind gets into quite a flurry!

The first thought is of a noble profession.
A dentist or a doctor could be an option!
But would I be able to stand the sight,
Of a human person's sickly insides?

I could maybe go down the technology way.
Be the cool coder who hasn't showered in days!
But what if it goes wrong, as programs often do!
Would I bring down a space shuttle or two?

Wouldn't it be great to stroll in a gallery,
That was filled with my creations, my artistry!
But that would need work, patience and time!
For at the moment, I can't even draw a line!

I could be a pilot or an astronaut!
To soar into space, now that's a thought!
But what if, I think with a frown,
I'm on the space shuttle that my code brought
down.

I could be a musician, was singing my calling?
Though at the moment it sounds like I'm just
bawling!
I could be an architect, designing buildings, tall!
But is it a sign that my toy blocks would always
fall?

I could make videos on Instagram and YouTube,
Telling people what to buy, which brand to
choose!
But then I look around and catch my father's
eye,
And quickly decide to let that idea slide.

Two whole minutes of silence, we've been this
way!
When the doorbell rings to save the day!
My best friend has come to say,
"Come on! It's time to play!"

I know I might seem rather immature!
But I promise I will be something for sure!
I don't know what, I don't know how.
But I just want to be a kid for now!

The Culinary Cooperative Society

Tara was sitting there, nose in her book.
She was in grade ten, where else would she
look?
She was at home, studying on her own,
When with hunger, she felt her tummy groan.

She lived in a building, that had ten flats,
Noisy kids, nosy aunties and all of that.
But they were kind and affectionate, all the
same.
Ready to help, if you even whispered their
names.

Coming back to the tale of Tara's hunger.
She looked at the empty fridge and began to
wonder,
How would she, her hunger allay,
When everyone who could cook was away!

She called her mom, ranting and fuming!
Her mom could think of a couple of things.
She told her to have a cup of instant soup,
And sent a message on the building's WhatsApp
group.

Soon at the door, stood Mrs. Vaidyanathan,
She lived on a lower floor, in flat number one.
An aroma wafted across, spicy and yum,
It came from a bowl of *idlis* and some steaming
rasam!

Of those cloud-like, soft *idlis*, Tara devoured
four!
A large helping of *rasam* and then some more.
As she drifted into bliss, she heard footsteps on
the floor,
Was that someone else at the door?

It was Paul, a Goan chef, new and budding,
He bore bebinca, a sticky, coconut, cake-like
pudding.
Excited, she cut herself a generous slice,
Licked her lips, and finished it in a trice!

She was about to slip into a fulfilled daze,
When another neighbour popped in, with what
she had made.
It was the shy and sweet Aisha Ansari,
Armed with a pot of fragrant *biryani*!

That *biryani* teased and tantalised!
Between a full stomach and greed, Tara
agonised.
The saffron rice and fried onions, sent her
straight to heaven!
But just then appeared Mr. Chatterjee from flat
number seven.

On his way back from a Bengali sweet shop,
At her place, he made a stop.
He handed her a box of *sondesh*, sweet and
luxurious,
The tiny bite she managed was simply delicious!

Knock! Knock! "Oh no! Please no more!"
Mrs. Khanna, from Punjab, was at the door.
She held a plate of Amritsari *kulcha* and *chhole*,
Tara took it, but ruefully saved it for the next
day!

Humbled and amazed, she was at how,
She had been flooded with sumptuous chow,

With the big-heartedness, love and generosity,
With Indian food and its tremendous diversity!

She learnt one more lesson that day,
That standing together was the only way.
Wherever you are from, wherever you did start,
All you need is a helping hand, and a warm
heart!

Sara's 'Cat'astrophe

Once to a wonderful magic show, Sara did go.
At the end, she was still rapt in thoughts of the
show.
A little boy came up to her and before she could
understand,
He had thrust a large bag into her unsuspecting
hand!

Before she knew it, he had disappeared into the
crowd,
There was nothing she could do, but take the bag
to her house.
Curious, she opened it, and almost fell back,
When out of the bag, slunk a green-eyed, black
cat.

As it ran out of the room, she caught a glimpse
of its back,
With a sigh of relief, she thought, "Ah! That's
that!"
Her friend Rhea's birthday was almost at hand.
She was meeting some friends, a surprise party
to plan.

They planned and happily conspired away,
Quickly hushing up, when Rhea came.
And then suddenly, simply out of the blue,
Sara blurted out, "We're planning a party for
you!"

She clapped her hands on her mouth, her friends
stared at her!
"Why would I do that?", she began to wonder!
What was going on? Why did she speak?
When she knew it was a wonderful secret to
keep?

Her class had an exam the next day, a nervous
silence fell.
Sara glanced at the paper, and knew she would
do well.
And then, suddenly, she slammed a hand on her
mouth,
But despite her attempt to stop, she shouted the
answers out!

What she had done was simply unbelievable!
Of keeping a secret, she was no longer capable!
She confided in her friends, they had to find a
solution.
To cure Sara's unimaginable condition!

They asked if anything had happened, that was
out of the ordinary.
Had she eaten or done something that was
different recently?
It came to her suddenly, in a big flash!
Did this have anything to do with the bag and
the cat?

Convinced this was the cause, they began to
search,
For that green-eyed, black cat, that had left Sara
in the lurch!
They looked everywhere, but in the pantry when
they peeped,
They found it curled up on the mat, fast asleep!

What next? They weren't sure. They didn't
know.
It struck them! Of course, in the bag it had to go!
They petted it, tempted it, how hard they tried,
Until, resignedly, it crawled inside!

They ran to the magic show, another victim to
find.
So that the bag and the cat could be left far
behind.
As for Sara, she is thankful and glad.
Never again, will she let a cat out of a bag!*

*Let the cat out of the bag is a popular idiom
that means to allow a secret to be known,
usually without intending to.

Numbers are ≠Heroes

"I hate Math." Do I hear you say?
From the sight of numbers, do you shy away?
But think for a moment, what life would be,
If numbers were eliminated completely!

Imagine that you're in a lift,
There are no numbers on the floors.
You just keep pressing up or down,
Until finally, you reach yours!

We've been using clocks for quite a while,
But without numbers, we would revert to a
sundial!
So if you were meeting someone for an evening
walk,
Would you say—"Let's meet at long-shadow
o'clock?"

Years ago, there was a way to gauge,
How old you were, what was your age.
All you did was put a stone in a box,
When the monsoon came, and down fell the
drops.

How old you were, you could see,
On whether the box was light or heavy.
But with climate change, the weather is bizarre,
Without dates, you would never know how old
you are!

You say it's not numbers that you hate.
It is the calculations that complicate!
But really would life be a smooth ride,
If there was no way to multiply and divide?

What if you had a cake recipe for three,
But you were baking for a party of more than
twenty.
About the number of eggs, would you
hypothesise?
And then pray to the cake, for it to rise?

On your birthday, for school, sweets you have
bought.
How many per person, you haven't really
thought.

You've given away plenty, been generous with
those chocs,
Now you're at the Principal's office, and there's
nothing in the box!

So embrace calculations, they're here to stay!
They're part of every hour of every day.
Even when you're thinking of 'nothing,' you
know,
'Nothing' after all is simply zero!

Don't Mind Your Own Buzzness

I am always there, always buzzing around,
When 'Thwack,' 'Humm,' 'Zzz', you hear such sounds,
Yes, I'm a housefly, as common as common can be,
I'm often told that there's nothing to like about me.

If I am so common, then why is this a story?
Because what happened one day was quite
extraordinary!
I was flying around, minding my own
'buzzness,'
When I entered a room where things looked
suspicious!

A motley group of people, hunched around a
table,
To come to an agreement, they seemed unable,
I sat on the rim of a cup, trying hard to surmise,
Wishing that I had compound ears and not
compound eyes.

They spoke of two sisters, who lived quite near,
But what they were saying made my heart freeze
with fear.
As I listened hard, shivers went down my wing.
This dreadful group of people was planning a
kidnapping!

Those two little girls, both sweet and kind,
Were going to be abducted, because they were
alone that night,
Their grandmother was famous, a rich business
tycoon,
And these evil people wanted a piece of her
fortune!

Furious, I had to act, on this piece of knowledge,
But I was just a two-bit fly, I didn't have the courage!
And then it came to me, a plan full of wonder,
'Cause though, as one, we were weak, we had strength in numbers.

I went to all my friends and asked each of them to find,
At least ten more flies, who would help us that night.
As evening approached, our troops began to form,
Just before twilight, of thousands, we were a swarm!

Outside the sisters' house they were ready in formation,
Waiting for my signal to begin the operation.
We were nervous, antennae cold and clammy,
But we were present, at every open nook and cranny!

"Go!" I said the word, and into the house we zoomed,
Looking for those two girls, we flew to every room.
We found them in the dining room, just about to eat,
Great! Along with saving them, we would also get a treat!

The swarm flew toward them, from each and every side,
They screamed and tried to swat us away, simply horrified!
I felt sorry for them, this would scare anyone.
But our goal was clear. Make them run!

We sat on their fingers, and arms and legs too,
We crawled over the dining table, and covered all their food!
Filled with disgust, they could stand no more!
Screaming and yelling, they raced out of the door!

We flew behind them, down the pathway,
Wanting to make sure that they ran far away!
As for the kidnappers, when in their car they came,
Greeted by the police, they had to give up their game!

The police had been called to solve the mystery of the flies!
But when they reached the house, there was not a fly in sight!
They were confused and surprised, but very thrilled to get,
Not flies, but kidnappers, caught in their net!

I feel much better now! Better self-esteem!
Even though I know that no one still likes me.
You see, it's nice to be important, stand big and tall,
But sometimes, it's more useful, to be a fly on the wall!*

Fly on the wall is a common idiom. If you say you want to be a fly on the wall, it means that you would like to hear what will be said or see what will happen, without being noticed.

The Red Car

I was waiting, washed and shiny!
Finally someone had decided to buy me!
I had been talked about, exhibited and shown.
And after all this time, they had found me a
home.

This couple, the cutest husband and wife.
Had just embarked on a new wedded life.
I vowed to always supply a comfy ride!
After all it was me, they'd be travelling inside!

Yes, I was a car, in a vibrant red!
When she saw me, the girl had said,
"This is the car in which I want to be."
"This is the perfect car for me!"

So they put their money together, all they had
saved.
Almost everything their jobs had made!
Adorned with a garland and a gorgeous bouquet,
It was she who drove me home that day!

I was with them as they had the time of their
lives,
Laughing and talking on so many drives!
Hills, narrow lanes and through big cities too,
I zipped along with all they did do!

I remember a day that was quite traumatic!
On a pole, a tiny part of me was nicked.
I was ok, would soon be out and about.
But the boy was upset and the girl cried her
heart out!

A day in my life, the most exciting,
Was when I was decorated in white and pink!
With embarrassment though I wanted to curl,
I brought home the most darling baby girl!

By now, I had a sibling, another new car!
A larger, silver, fancy Honda!
But it was still me that brought home the second
bundle of joy,
The cutest, round, little baby boy!

The next few years were full of frolic and fun!
The family folks were always on the run!
On picnics, school drops and to classes we went!
To ferry them around, on me they did depend!

How the years went by, time flew!
A couple of years were spent during Covid too!
I just sat, languishing away.
With nowhere to go, day after day!

Soon I was out again, but now quite old!
Would I be kept? Would I be sold?
Suddenly, without warning, came the day.
When by a stranger I was driven away.

"That's not fair!" I wanted to bawl!
I should break down or let my engine stall!
But all I did was take the chance,
To give my home of fifteen years, one last
glance.

Was I being taken to a junk or scrap yard?
Oh! What's this? It looks like a garage!
And then I realised—it's not what it seems!
I was getting an overhaul—of any car's dreams!

My engine was tuned, I had a new clutch!
A coat of paint, and a music system that I loved
so much!
I arrived home, spanking new!
In my heart was a big thank you!

Although I'm not out much now.
There's something I do realise!
That they are not a family of four,
But we are a family of five!

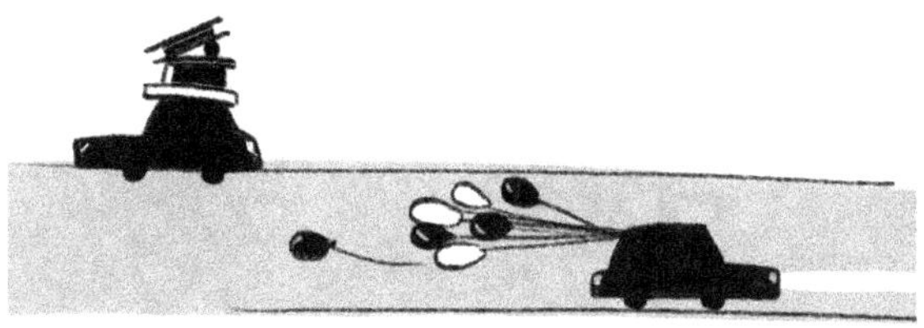

The 'Gut'sy Journey

I am a morsel, a morsel of food,
Food like a pizza, that tastes so good.
But do you know what a mess I become?
Once you put me in your mouth,
And I slip past your tongue?

Here's a look at my journey,
A little insight!
As through your Digestive System,
I take a long ride!

You simply put me in your mouth,
And enjoy the taste.
But have you spared a thought,
For the troubles I've faced?

Your teeth slam into me,
They tear, chew, grind and blitz.
Until I am nothing but...
A clump of tiny little bits.

I am now taken over,
With a flood of something new!
Something wet and slimy,
It's saliva! Yes, your drool!
But the saliva actually helps me slide and slip,
Into your throat, I now drip!

Here, there is a point where two tubes meet!
The tube with air that you breathe,
And the tube with food that you eat.
And if it were not for a little flap,
That covers the air tube just like a cap,
Into the air tube I could sneak off,
And make you sputter and make you cough!

Now I travel into the depths of you!
It is the stomach that I have come to,
The stomach is strong and made of muscle,
I'm thrown about, a-churn and all a-tussle!

And just when I think, I can handle no more!
I notice there's something more in store!
Something that oozes from your stomach's wall,
It's acid, that kills germs, bacteria and all!

I'm no longer bread, cheese and things like that!
I'm all vitamins and carbs and proteins and fat!
And into you deeper, as I go,
These goodies in me, come to the fore!
It is these goodies that you need, you know,
To make you strong, to help you grow!

Downward and onward to the small intestine,
Why do they call it small? Your guess is as good
as mine!
'Cause a small intestine isn't all that small!
Uncoiled and held up, it would be 22 feet tall!

Friends of the small intestine,
the gallbladder, pancreas and liver,
Are so very generous digestive juice givers,
With their help, the small intestine does extract,
Every nutrient with which I was packed!

Into your blood, the goodies slip,
Across your bodies they start to spread,
I'm in your leg, your nose, your lip!
Me, who was just a humble piece of bread!

And what happens to the rest of the goop?
Yes, it has turned into lots of poop!
Into your large intestine it goes, that mush,
And finally goes, right down the flush!

Rodent in Residence

I am just a plain house mouse.
But a real smart cookie,
Quick and nimble on my feet,
And as clever as clever can be!

One day, I was scampering about,
Of course, looking for some food.
When suddenly, I was enveloped in a smell,
A smell that smelled so good!

I started going toward that smell,
As if in a trance.
And then to slip into a kitchen,
I got a golden chance!
The window had been left open,
Open, just a crack!

But a crack is more than enough,
When a mouse wants a snack!

That night, I was king of the kitchen,
To every corner did I go!
Devouring everything in sight,
Except for half a potato!

That potato gave the game away,
It was not my fault!
When the family spotted it half-eaten,
My plundering came to a halt!

They spotted my droppings everywhere!
On many a-vessel, pan and pot!
Sorry, but when a mouse is excited,
Control himself, he cannot!

The family readied for battle,
With gloves, sticks and a broom.
They closed all the doors,
So I could not escape the room!

I crept into a corner,
Absolutely still, I stayed
Not a whisker did I move,
Not a single sound I made!
I saw them yank the cupboards open,
And push the trolleys away,

After looking hard, they shouted—
"The mouse has gone! Yay!"

Man and mouse lived happily,
And peace did prevail,
Until I made the grave mistake,
Of letting them spot my tail!

The family smartened up,
And changed tack and gear,
Those tempting jars, those tasty crumbs,
Began to disappear!

In a matter of minutes,
The whole kitchen was bare!
Words like mouse trap and medicine,
Were hanging in the air!

I cannot believe these humans!
They need to get an update!
After all these years, can medicine and traps,
Really still exterminate?

The bait was there, the trap was set,
I went to examine it,
It was quite well set up,
And I was tempted, I'll admit.

I nibbled at the bait,
A deliciously sugary tomato,
But once I had gobbled it up,
Near the trap I did not go!

But now another problem,
Loomed its head up high!
Food was so very scarce,
That I would soon become weak and die!

I had to make an escape,
But how? All was sealed!
For any crack or slit,
I kept my eyes peeled!

But my captors were thorough,
An exit, there was none!
Slowly out of my body,
I felt my energy run.

I needed to use my wit,
To get out of this place.
I needed to see my captors,
Meet them face to face!

The next morning, I pretended,
To be paralyzed in fear!
I stayed out in the open,
Even when my captors came near!

I felt a flash of panic
When I saw the raised broom,
But thankfully they used it,
To escort me from the room.

Oh! To be in the drains again!
Oh! To be free!
To see the sights and smell the smells
That were so familiar to me!

Now finally, I can sit back,
And think about the chase,
The day I got the better of,
Some members of the human race!

Frivolous Fighting

My sister and I had a fight!
She was wrong and I was right!
Fists flew, it was quite a brawl.
Grr! Why do siblings exist at all!

She's furious, 'cause at her I threw a sock!
It's just a piece of cloth, and not a rock!
And after all, it's just not fair!
For her to put it on MY chair!

But that's not how it began, you see!
Wait till you hear what she did to me!
I know she'd get mad, she'd feel the pinch!
If it were her books, that had been moved by one inch!

For a while our battle went unresolved.
And then of course, the parents got involved!
This generally worked for me,
I was younger and went scot-free!

This time too, it was just the same!
It was she, getting all the blame!
I was getting the revenge I knew I should!
But wondering why I wasn't feeling good!

Once our parents had left,
She sat quietly, looking quite bereft!
A contemptuous glance she threw at me!
I felt a new feeling—a wee bit sorry!

This was a problem, something was amiss!
I couldn't go on feeling like this!
She had always loved my electric sharpener,
So I picked it up and gave it to her.

She looked at me, in complete surprise.
Was this what I was willing to sacrifice?
On her face, spread a small smile.
All was well with the world for a while!

But suddenly she spied, above the bed,
Her poster on which I had scribbled in red!
Time to run away, time to flee!
In desperate need of my safety!

The Sidewalk Story - Discovery

This is the first of two poems that tells the story of a child who encounters two children who live on the street.

I was walking back from school one day,
Soon I would go out with my friends to play,
Then I would head home; and get well-fed,
And soon after, I would fall into my cosy bed.

Just then I happened to catch sight,
Of a girl and a boy walking on my right.
They found something funny, and soon after,
Burst into peals and peals of laughter.

Curiosity overcame me, I had to see,
What it was that they found so funny,
But as I looked at them with
wide-open eyes,
A lot of things took me by
surprise.

Their clothes looked dirty, and quite bedraggled.
Their faces were grimy, their hair lay straggled.
Some buttons were undone, they had no shoes
on their feet.
They looked like they hadn't had much to eat.

They caught me staring and all of us froze.
I was lost for words, though I'm quite verbose.
And then they came, one after another,
All those questions that made me wonder.

"Where are you from? Where do you stay?"
"Without washing your face, did your parents let
you get away?"
"Your dress has spots, his shirt is torn"
"Why on your feet, no shoes have you worn!"

They looked startled and ashamed a bit.
But still I did not let go of it.
I knew their privacy I had invaded,
I saw that now their smiles had faded.

"Down that road," the boy said. "Just over
there."
I couldn't see a building or a bungalow
anywhere.
I asked if they would walk down with me,
To show me the house that I just couldn't see.

Pots were being washed, a baby was crying,
On one side, a man was just lying.
We walked a little further, down that street,
And stopped before a tent-like, blue, plastic
sheet.

This was their home? Without even a door?
With flies buzzing everywhere and garbage on
the floor?
With mice scampering about and roaches too!
Is this the place where they lived, these two?

Suddenly I don't know what came over me.
I knew from this place, I had to flee!
No longer this street, could I roam.
I ran away to the comfort of my home.

The Sidewalk Story - Understanding

*If you haven't read 'The Sidewalk Story -
Discovery' yet, do read it before reading this
poem.*

That night, I kept tossing and turning,
With so many questions, my mind was burning.
Would they have crawled into their plastic
house?
Were they fast asleep next to a roach or mouse?

I wanted to visit them, wanted to know.
Back to their home, I wanted to go.
I shouldn't have, so cowardly, run away,
So I decided to go the very next day!

The boy was sitting on the edge of the footpath.
He looked like he had just finished his bath.
"Where's the bathroom? From where does the
water come?"
He pointed at water filled in a large drum.

As I looked at it with surprise and doubt,
A woman dipped in a vessel, and took some out.
She poured it into a bowl of uncooked rice.
With the same water, she was making a 'pulao'
that night!

The girl now came along, as usual, smiling.
She was busy playing with a bit of string.
I asked her, of toys, did she have a hoard?
She brought out a box made of cardboard.

I looked as she opened it, eager to see,
All the things that must keep her busy.
Two sticks, some stones and a button or two,
A broken pencil, a marble and the lace of a shoe.

I asked if they had had some lunch.
They said they had got two biscuits to munch.
Looking at my expression, they rushed to
reassure,
That they would have some dinner for sure.

When I asked about school, they swelled with
pride.
"Most times we go by rickshaw," they replied.
Only sometimes, just once in a while.
They had to walk back the two and a half miles.

Everybody is different and so are their
circumstances.
Everybody in life gets a varied set of chances.
Though it's very different, where the two of
them stay,
Maybe, just maybe I can help them someday.

One thing though, I'm happy about,
Is that, very often, when I go out,
I see that pair, playing together,
Giggling, smiling and laughing as ever!

Bedtime Battles

Sleeping is such a waste of time!
There is so much to do on this day of mine.
Books to read and games to play,
It's way too early to call it a day.

It's 9:00 pm, but the house is still a-buzz.
Then for just me to sleep, why all the fuss?
Stop nagging me for heaven's sake!
In all this activity, I want to partake!

I made a paper rocket earlier today.
Does it soar, or does its flight fail?
It will only take two minutes, I beg and pray!
Tomorrow is just too far away!

Oh and in class, I learnt a football trick.
You have to see it now, it is just epic!
I worked at it hard, made so many tries,
I ask you to see it, with beseeching eyes!

I show you the trick, finish other things on my
list.
Towards my room, I slowly start to drift.
Suddenly my heart sinks, I see danger lurk!
I've forgotten to do my maths homework!

An hour has gone by, the deadline missed.
Your eyes have narrowed, your voice is clipped.
I'm almost ready to put up my feet.
I only have to brush my teeth!

I'm snuggled up in my warm, cosy bed.
On the cool pillow, I rest my head.
I risk a question as I peep through the sheets,
Didn't you say I should always read before I
sleep?

The Face Wash

Young Aadit once had a dream!
That an old woman gave him a bottle of cream!
But it wasn't a dream he realised because,
In the morning he saw a bottle, though, of face
wash!

Waking up, still rubbing his eyes,
To the kitchen he strolled, just outside.
"Oh no!" He scowled. *Dosas* for breakfast!
For something more exciting he wished!

With the new soap, he washed his face,
And then at the dining table, took his place.

It lay on his plate—hot, crisp and caramelised!
Three luscious chutneys were on the side.
With hunger, the sight made his tummy roar!
Was this the same *dosa* he spurned, moments
before!

At school were two history classes, back to
back!
He yawned and thought—"What a drag!"
He excused himself and went to the loo!
Hoping to miss at least a minute or two!

With the new soap, he washed his face,
And then back in class, he took his place.

The warriors in his book came alive before his
eyes!
He saw the valour with which they had lived and
died!
Their battles were fascinating, strategic but
devious!
Had he really thought history was boring and
tedious?

He got home to see his mom on a work call.
She was always busy, never free at all!
On the bus, he got so sticky and hot!
But pick him up from school, she just would
not!

With the new soap, he washed his face,
And then in his mom's study, he found some
space.

He watched her, being cool and confident.
And as her work she did present,
He heard the cheers and applause loud!
He felt goosebumps all over, and so very proud!

With the new soap, as he washed his face,
He pondered on the twists that had taken place.
And there it was, right before his eyes!
The face wash concoction had made him realise—
Thinking in a way that was a little different,
Could make the world appear simply magnificent!

My Favourite Things Today

You can sing this to the tune of the original song.

Swanky new phones, and new hi-tech laptops!
Not talking to people, interacting with chatbots!
Playing games on my mobile, every evening!
These are a few of my favourite things!

Reels on the gram, and movies on Netflix!
Videos on YouTube or Prime Video top picks!
Using Spotify to hear someone sing!
These are a few of my favourite things!

For Roblox or Minecraft, going online,
Scrolling through SnapChat, wasting my time!
Waiting and waiting for my phone to ping!
These are a few of my favourite things!

When the net is down,
When the phone dies!
When I'm feeling sad.
I simply remember my favourite things and then
I take out….my iPad!

Taking the Plunge

Rohit was a great dancer, and boy, could he sing!
At any exam he seemed to know, simply
everything!
At a game of kabaddi, no one could defeat him.
But there was one thing he couldn't do—he just
couldn't swim.

There was a small pond, in his picturesque little
town.
In which his friends would swim and splash and
simply play around.
They told him to glide in, let the water flow over
his head.
But he would start to panic and it would enter
his nose instead!

An event was held each year, open to all schools
in the state.
It was a contest—a running, cycling, swimming
race.
Rohit's school had a chance this year, a golden
opportunity!
They had a team that could defeat any team from
the city!

Rohit was not a part of it, for he could not swim.
But that didn't stop him from cheering for his
friends to win!
The team practised hard, prepped themselves for
the day.
But a calamity befell them on the morning of the
race.

One of the participants, the star of the show.
Tripped while running down the stairs and broke
his little toe.
Though it was a small crack, he could not cycle,
swim or run.
And it now fell on Rohit, for besides him there
was none!

Rohit broke into a sweat, as dread filled his
heart.

But he smiled at his teammates as he lined up to start.
He was confident in all but the last part of the race.
Where he would have to swim across a segment of a lake.

He breezed through the cycle ride and the ten-kilometre run too.
But now his legs shook as at the edge of the lake he stood.
He was in the lead so far, but now felt under the pump.
As the crowd cheered him on, urging him to jump.

He waded into the water and took a deep breath.
To kick his feet off the ground, he tried to get set.
As the water flowed over his head, a cold panic gripped him.
He wondered what in the world he was doing, knowing he couldn't swim.

He thrashed about a bit, arms and legs flailing,
He felt as though he was drowning, at this task
he was failing!
He stood up once again, told himself to get a
grip.
He willed himself to calm down and took a
second dip.

To all thoughts of drowning, he closed his mind
tight.
He kept only his target—the opposite shore, in
sight.
He tried to stay calm, moved his arms and legs
in rhythm.
And tried to disregard the opponent that crossed
him.

He reached the other end and heaved a sigh of
relief.
They hadn't won the race, or so he believed.
But as he got out of the water, he realised that
wasn't it.
The triathlon ended with a hundred-metre sprint!

He scrambled to his feet with a grin of delight.
For a hundred-metre sprint, he could put up a
great fight.
He gave it his very best, and as he reached the
end.

In the nick of time, he crossed his opponent.

He went to bed that night with a smile on his
face.
Not only because they won the triple race.
Though he never would be the best swimmer
ever,
At the mere sight of the water, now never would
he shiver.

Horror-struck

I was once invited to a party for Halloween,
I was a bit wary and not very keen.
But in a little fun, there was nothing wrong,
So I set off, when the shadows grew long.

The minute I got there, I felt a vibe.
Cold and chilly and not very nice.
I was being silly, there was nothing to fear!
It was all fake, this scary atmosphere!

We were playing and laughing, all us kids.
When suddenly it grew cold, almost frigid!
We felt a sharp, biting gust of wind.
And then it was gone, in just a second!

What was that? What could it be?
We looked around with uncertainty.
Why did that phantom wind blow that night?
Has someone unknown got an invite?

Soon it was time for some juice and snacks.
That put the party back on track!
But just as soon as we picked them up,
Something sticky and green was dripping from
the cups!

We shrieked! This is not imagination!
This better have some explanation!
We asked the cook, but she only said,
She had poured cranberry juice, that was red!

The green thing spread as we watched terrified!
Our feet were on the sofa, many of us cried!
It bubbled and oozed and spread some more!
Until it all but covered the floor!

Suddenly within it an image did appear!
The face of a girl, twisted with fear!
Eyes were wide, a mask of terror she wore!
Suddenly it hardened, cracked and disappeared
into the floor!

Horrorstruck, with fear we were fraught!
It was that face that filled our thoughts!
All we wanted was to get away!
And never return to that frightful place!

We tried and tried, but it wouldn't budge, the
door.
And then we noticed some gift bags on the floor.
Maybe we were supposed to pick one each,
And only then this door we could breach!

It worked! The door opened, we rushed out!
I didn't stop running till I reached my house!
The gift bag that I held in my hand,
On the way, I tossed and ran!

Reached home and suddenly, out loud I cried!
For on the table, the bag I spied!
That same, dumped gift bag of mine!
And it had a jar of that sticky green slime!

The Case of the Missing Stripes

In the African Savannah,
Not far from Nairobi,
There lived a herd of zebras,
As happy as can be.

In the day, on the generous Savannah,
They would roam free and graze,
But when the sun went down, and night fell,
They would lie back, relax and laze!

But one day something happened,
Quite out of the ordinary,
It made them prick up their ears,
It made them scared and wary.

They went out as usual,
At the crack of dawn,
And decided to head home,
When the babies began to yawn!

Suddenly, from the middle,
Of the galloping herd,
There rose a cry of fear,
All the zebras were disturbed!

In their midst, there stood,
In the fading evening light,
A zebra, proud and tall,
With not a single stripe in sight!

The other zebras gathered around,
Their mouths open wide,
Who was this dark stranger
That no one could recognize?

Within the herd, should they let him stay?
Or should the young stallions drive him away?
Was he a danger, was he a threat?
Or had he just not got his stripes as yet?

The wise, old zebras had a talk.
And at the end, they did concur,
That the morning would bring a solution,
So they let the stranger sleep over.

As the morning came, they heard,
Galloping that sounded like thunder!
The zebras awoke, afraid!
And looked at each other in wonder!

On the horizon, in a cloud of dust,
Shapes began to appear.
The zebras pawed the ground anxiously,
As the shapes drew nearer!

And then, the zebras,
Could hardly believe their eyes!
In front of them, stood more zebras,
But again, with just no stripes!

Suddenly the dark stranger,
The visitor of the night before,
Let out a delighted whinny,
And cantered to the fore!

He turned back and tossed his mane,
And then trotted across the grass.
To join the others who looked like him,
The team of stripeless zebras!

They then turned and galloped away,
Toward the watering hole,
That family of wild horses,
That came looking for their missing foal!

Dear Drop

This "Save water" business is such a pain!
I have been told, over and over again,
Save water you must! Save every drop!
Or else, our water supply will eventually stop!

This statement I just don't believe!
Cities get flooded with the rain we receive!
Of water there is absolutely no dearth!
I've learnt that it covers more than seventy
percent of the Earth!

For my bath I was asked to use water in one
bucket.
But I shut the bathroom door and well did I lock
it!
I then spent almost over an hour,
Feeling the hot water gush from the shower!

March brought with it, the festival of colour.
In two hours, we were covered with psychedelic
powder!
It was hot, so to get ourselves cool,
We leapt into the giant, community swimming
pool!

Later we looked at the water, a little guilty and
wide-eyed!
But it was just once in a year, we justified!
They couldn't clean it, the water treaters.
And they drained it away, all sixty thousand
litres!

The committee raised a big hue and cry!
They made such a hullabaloo! But why?
This issue I needed to understand and
appreciate!
I think I needed to get an update!

Though the percentage of water on Earth is
seventy-one,
Most of it is in salty oceans, usable by none!
Three percent remains, of which frozen water is
more than two!
Less than one percent remains for people like
me and you!

Of that one percent water, that seems to be
around,
More than two-thirds is deep underground!
The amount of nice, fresh water stored in lakes,
Is a measly percent of zero point zero zero eight!

The water situation is dire indeed!
Of saving it, there is every need!
But even if one bucket a day I save,
How would it solve a problem, so big and
grave?

It's not just me, it's a numbers game!
For if every child were to do the same,
We would save so much water and then some!
It would last us for generations to come!

Mamma

Dedicated to my mamma, my friend forever.

Just the way every lock, has only one key,
Our mums were made for us, very specially.
God knew our characters, and what we would
be,
And then made yours for you and made mine for
me.

The day you were born, she held you very tight.
And she lay that way, late into the night.
She swore to herself that against any odds, she
would fight.
She would fiercely protect you, with all her
might.

As you grew stronger, her love grew with you.
She could never stop talking about all that you
would do.

As your needs increased and you started school,
She slowly shaped her life, entirely around you.

Your mamma may have been at home, and spent
the day with you,
Your mamma may have gone to work, like many
mammas do.
Wherever she was, you simply cannot question
That you were always, the centre of her
attention.

Whenever something good you do, she will
swell with pride.
If you make a mistake or flounder, it will be
justified.
She may never say it to your face, that I can't
deny.
But say it to you or not, you're the apple of her
eye.

Of course, she'll yell at you, give you a piece of
her mind.
But one thing you must remember—she's being
cruel to be kind.
For the world is quite dangerous, a difficult
place,
And she's toughening you up, in a sheltered
space.

Those kisses and embraces, little gestures of
love.
Don't turn your face away, or say I've had
enough.
For when she comes up and tightly hugs you,
I'll let you in on a secret—she needs a hug too!

So although today you may be, at loggerheads
with your mamma,
Things will change, and soon, will end all this
drama.
There will come a time, when she becomes your
friend.
And you will treasure the relationship right up to
the end.